rain clouds

Meerabai

translated by

Subhash Jaireth

rain clouds
Recent Work Press
Canberra, Australia

Translation copyright © Subhash Jaireth, 2020

ISBN: 9780648834328(paperback)

 A catalogue record for this book is available from the National Library of Australia

All rights reserved. This book is copyright. Except for private study, research, criticism or reviews as permitted under the Copyright Act, no part of this book may be reproduced, stored in a retrieval system, or transmitted in any form by any means without prior written permission. Enquiries should be addressed to the publisher.

Cover image: Valery Rabchenyuk on unsplash
Cover design: Recent Work Press
Set by Recent Work Press

recentworkpress.com

SS

to Hanna

Introductory Note

Meerabai (1498-1556) was a poet, singer and dancer and a devotee of Hindu god Krishna. She is revered as one of the prominent voices of the Bhakti Movement: a movement of religious reformation which valued personal engagement with deities over traditional ritualistic practices.

Her life and work are shrouded in mystery, clouded by legends, gossip and stories. She is said to have been born in 1498 (or 1502) into a minor royal family in Marwar, Rajasthan in north-west India. When she was five, her mother died, and she was brought up by her grandfather. At the age of eighteen, or perhaps younger, she was given away in marriage to the crown-prince of a neighbouring kingdom. She found married life oppressive and wanted instead to devote her life to Lord Krishna, who she believed was her true husband. She composed songs in his praise and sang them in temples dancing in ecstasy and rapture.

Both her husband, and her father-in-law, the King, found her behaviour scandalous, and declared her either insane or a woman of loose morals who had brought shame to the royal family. After the death of her husband (in 1523) and father-in-law (in 1528), other members of the royal family continued to persecute her. There are stories that they tried more than once to kill her by feeding her poison. She survived and left the royal home, turning into a *yogin*, a religious mendicant. She travelled to places associated with Krishna, either alone or in the company of other devotees, singing and dancing with them. Life around her was in turmoil, with frequent wars waged by the Hindu kingdom either among each other, or against the Muslim rulers. Her songs of love and peace, sung in the glory of her Krishna, sounded as moments of respite from the endless violence happening around her.

**

Like most Indians, I have grown up reading and listening to her songs. They have been recorded by Indian classical vocalists and by several popular Bollywood singers and musicians. They are sung everywhere: in temples, music festivals and in films. Her life has been turned into feature films, dance dramas, and plays.

Most of her songs remained unwritten in her lifetime and were transmitted orally. It's quite likely that some were edited and embellished in the process. It is equally possible that some of the songs attributed to her were composed by other poets.

Meerabai composed her songs in the language she spoke and heard which includes words from several local Rajasthani dialects. She also used words from Braj Bhasha, a language spoken in north-central India. Over time these dialects and languages evolved to form Hindi or Hindustani, a language presently spoken by a large majority of people in north India.

Meerabai composed her songs so that they could be sung aloud. This is what controls their meter and rhythm. The two also help a performer to dance to and with them.

The rhythm is created by various types of end-rhymes as well by the meter. The most common rhyme pattern used is AA, BA, CA, DA etc. Some songs use a single end-rhyme pattern AA.

Like most poets of her time, she inserts her name in the final couplet of the song. This introduces a third-person voice in the songs, creating an impression that the poet wants to speak to herself as the other. Most poems are addressed to her lover, her Lord Krishna, for whom she employs different names: *Girdhar*, *Dark-skinned*, *Hari*, and *Govinda*. In some songs the addressee is either her mother or her girl-friends.

In most songs addressed to Krishna, Meerabai confesses that she loves her Krishna so much that she is ready to die for him. However, there are songs in which she performs the role of a disappointed and jilted lover, ready to throw a tantrum.

Meerabai also finds a place for the male members of her royal family. They are all represented by Ranaji, a proxy either of her husband or her father-in-law.

**

Translating the love songs of Meerabai into English presents a challenge, and the challenge lies in achieving the right balance between the meaning, mood and the soundscape of these intensely sonorous songs.

As I began translating them, I first tried to reproduce their end-rhyme pattern in English. But I soon discovered that the such a translation sounded laboured, contrived and unnatural. This forced me to focus on the rhythm instead, and to use rhyme flexibly and floatingly.

In my translation I have tried my best to preserve the number of lines. In a few songs this hasn't been easy because the language of the original is so precise and measured that I needed more words to convey the meaning and the mood.

Meerabai is known to have composed thousands of songs. The fifteen songs I have translated represent a mere drop in that large ocean.

—*Subhash Jaireth, 2020*

References

Martin, N. 2010, 'Meerabai Comes to America: The Translation and Transformation of a Saint', *The Journal of Hindu Studies*, vol. 3, 12-35.

Sangari, K. 1990, 'Meerabai and the Spiritual Economy of Bhakti', Part One, *Economic and Political Weekly*, vol. 25, no. 27, 1464-1475.

Sangari, K. 1990, 'Meerabai and the Spiritual Economy of Bhakti', Part Two, *Economic and Political Weekly*, vol. 25, no. 28, 1537-1541 + 1543-1545 + 1547-1552.

Meerabai, Poems, at Kavita-Kosh (Library of Poems), in Hindi, http://kavitakosh.org/kk/%E0%A4%AE%E0%A5%80%E0%A4%B0%E0%A4%BE%E0%A4%AC%E0%A4%BE%E0%A4%88, accessed in December 2019.

(1)

बरसै बदरिया सावन की,
सावन की मनभावन की ।
सावन में उमग्यो मेरो मनवा,
भनक सुनी हरि आवन की ॥
उमड घुमड चहुं दिस से आयो,
दामण दमके झर लावन की ।
नान्हीं नान्हीं बूंदन मेहा बरसै,
सीतल पवन सुहावन की ॥
मीरा के प्रभु गिरधर नागर,
आनन्द मंगल गावन की ॥

(1)

They are raining, the dark
clouds of *savan* my love.
The *savan* that fills my
heart with joy my love.
It misses a beat hearing you are
about to knock on my door love.
The clouds, thick and heavy
come raining, wetting the hem
of my colourful skirt my love.
The rain drops softly, the breeze
is cool, its touch like you my love.
You are Girdhar my Lord, I say, and
can't stop singing your praises my love.

(2)

हेरी म्हा दरद दिवाणौ
म्हारा दरद ना जाण्याँ कोय ।
घायल री गत घायल जाण्याँ
हिबडो अगण संजोय ॥
जौहर की गत जौहरी जाणै
क्या जाण्याँ जण खोय
मीरा री प्रभु पीर मिटाँगा
जब वैद साँवरो होय ॥

(2)

Look how love is hurting me my friend,
and no one has the heart to see the flame
burning me; they aren't wounded as I am,
and they don't have the eye of a jeweller
who can spot a gem and keep it safe.
Look how love is hurting me my friend;
my pain, says Meera, will only wane when my dark-
skinned Lord, my healer, has come to me to rain.

(3)

म्हारे घर आओ प्रीतम प्यारा।।
तन मन धन सब भेंट धरूंगी भजन करूंगी तुम्हारा।
म्हारे घर आओ प्रीतम प्यारा।।
तुम गुणवंत सुसाहिब कहिये मोमें औगुण सारा।।
म्हारे घर आओ प्रीतम प्यारा।।
मैं निगुणी कछु गुण नहिं जानूं तुम सा बगसणहारा।।
म्हारे घर आओ प्रीतम प्यारा।।
मीरा कहै प्रभु कब रे मिलोगे तुम बिन नैण दुखारा।।
म्हारे घर आओ प्रीतम प्यारा।।

(3)

Come to my house, my darling love;
to feast on my body, heart and wealth
and I'll sing hymns in your praise.
Come to my house, my darling love;
you are unblemished the sages say
and I'm weak, flawed and truculent.
Come to my house, my darling love;
I'm dull, plain and ignorant whereas
you are virtuous, wise, and impeccable.
Come to my house, my darling love,
says Meera, my eyes are tired
waiting to gaze at your blessed face.
Come to my house my darling love.

(4)

मैं तो सांवरे के रंग राची।
साजि सिंगार बांधि पग घुंघरू, लोक-लाज तजि नाची।।
गई कुमति, लई साधुकी संगति, भगत, रूप भै सांची।
गाय गाय हरिके गुण निस दिन, कालब्यालसूँ बांची।।
उण बिन सब जग खारो लागत, और बात सब कांची।
मीरा श्रीगिरधरन लालसूँ भगति रसीली जांची।।

(4)

I've dyed myself dark to look like you;
bejewelled and painted I dance with
anklet bells, ignoring shame and honour.
I have lost my mind, befriended sadhus,
and have turned into your crazy slave.
I sing, my Hari, your praises day and
night forgetting place and time.
Without you the world is bland, and
words brittle like tinted glassy chimes.
I yearn for you my Girdhar, sings Meera,
my love is infinite, and my faith divine.

(5)

हरि मेरे जीवन प्राण अधार।
और आसरो नांही तुम बिन, तीनू लोक मंझार॥
हरि मेरे जीवन प्राण अधार
आपबिना मोहि कछु न सुहावै निरख्यौ सब संसार।
हरि मेरे जीवन प्राण अधार
मीरा कहै मैं दासि रावरी, दीज्यो मती बिसार॥
हरि मेरे जीवन प्राण अधार।

(5)

Hari you are my saviour,
without you I've no home, no bearing.
Hari you are my saviour,
without you my world is dull and dreary.
Hari you are my saviour,
without you I go crazy,
says Meera, alarmed that you'll forget me.
Hari you are my saviour.

(6)

तनक हरि चितवौ जी मोरी ओर।
हम चितवत तुम चितवत नाहीं
    मन के बड़े कठोर।
मेरे आसा चितनि तुम्हरी
    और न दूजी ठौर।
तुमसे हमकूँ एक हो जी
    हम-सी लाख करोर।।
कब की ठाड़ी अरज करत हूँ
    अरज करत भै भोर।
मीरा के प्रभु हरि अबिनासी
    देस्यूँ प्राण अकोर।।

(6)

Look at me just once, just once, my love.
I look at you and you turn away,
    you are truly heartless, my love.
My hopes hinge on your single glance
    you are my true haven, my love.
I've only you and no one else whereas there
    are many like me for you, my love.
I plead and pray each night till the very dawn,
    hollow and hopeless, my love.
You are Meera's almighty Lord, for you I am
    ready to give up my life, my love.

(7)

गली तो चारों बंद हुई, मैं हरिसे मिलूं कैसे जाय।
ऊंची नीची राह लपटीली, पांव नहीं ठहराय।
सोच सोच पग धरूं जतनसे, बार बार डिग जाय॥
ऊंचा नीचा महल पियाका म्हांसूं चढ्यो न जाय।
पिया दूर पंथ म्हारो झीणो, सुरत झकोला खाय॥
कोस कोस पर पहरा बैठ्या, पैंड़ पैंड़ बटमार।
है बिधना, कैसी रच दीनी दूर बसायो म्हांरो गांव॥
मीरा के प्रभु गिरधर नागर सतगुरु दई बताय।
जुगन जुगन से बिछड़ी मीरा घर में लीनी लाय॥

(7)

All streets to my Hari are blocked, and I can't find my way to him.

The winding track goes up and down, and my feet slide and slip
I walk each step with caution, and yet I constantly trip and fall.

The palace where my love resides sits high on a hill, and the climb
is arduous; my love is far away, his face forgotten, his smile mislaid.

At each stop stands an armed guard, and each step I take is onerous;
the fate has dealt me the roughest deal by sending my love so far away.

The Lord of Meera is Girdhar, her true guru says, but year after year
she lives without him by her side; her house is empty, her life no life.

(8)

पग घूँघरू बाँध मीरा नाची रे।
मैं तो मेरे नारायण की आपहि हो गई दासी रे।
लोग कहै मीरा भई बावरी न्यात कहै कुलनासी रे॥
विष का प्याला राणाजी भेज्या पीवत मीरा हाँसी रे।
मीरा के प्रभु गिरिधर नागर सहज मिले अविनासी रे॥

(8)

Meera has put on the anklet bells, ready to dance for her Lord, turning herself into his crazy slave. You've lost your mind, the people say; you've brought us shame, the family cries. I drank poison from Ranaji's chalice, and didn't I laugh and laugh? I thought he knew, my only Lord is Girdhar; he is my saviour, my love, my blessed light.

(9)

राणोजी रूठे तो म्हारो कांई करसी,
म्हे तो गोविन्दरा गुण गास्याँ हे माय।।
राणोजी रूठे तो अपने देश रखासी,
म्हे तो हरि रूठ्यां रूठे जास्याँ हे माय।
लोक-लाजकी काण न राखाँ,
म्हे तो निर्भय निशान गुरास्याँ हे माय।
राम नाम की जहाज चलास्याँ,
म्हे तो भवसागर तिर जास्याँ हे माय।
हरिमंदिर में निरत करास्या,
म्हे तो घूघरिया छमकास्याँ हे माय।
चरणामृत को नेम हमारो,
म्हे तो नित उठ दर्शण जास्याँ हे माय।
मीरा गिरधर शरण सांवल के,
म्हे ते चरण-कमल लिपरास्यां हे माय।

(9)

It isn't my fault that Ranaji sulks.
He sulks because I sing praises of
Govinda, my true love, mother.
He sulks and tells me he'll send me
away, but doesn't he know that
I can't let my Hari grumble, mother.
I have no ears to hear that I've lost
shame and pride because I am
fearless, ready to seize whatever
catches my fickle fancy, mother.
The ship I have got on board
is called Ram, sailing to the far
shore of the worldly ocean, mother.
I dance in the temple of Hari,
my anklets jingle and jangle, mother.
I drink his nectar, and crave to gaze at
his face every other minute, mother.
He is my refuge, my dark-skinned
Girdhar, to wrap around his lotus feet
is my will, and chosen fate, mother.

(10)

दूर नगरी, बड़ी दूर नगरी-नगरी
कैसे मैं तेरी गोकुल नगरी
दूर नगरी बड़ी दूर नगरी
रात को कान्हा डर माही लागे,
दिन को तो देखे सारी नगरी। दूर नगरी...
सखी संग कान्हा शर्म मोहे लागे,
अकेली तो भूल जाऊँ तेरी डगरी। दूर नगरी...
धीरे-धीरे चलूँ तो कमर मोरी लचके
झटपट चलूँ तो छलकाए गगरी। दूर नगरी...
मीरा कहे प्रभु गिरधर नागर,
तुमरे दरस बिन मैं तो हो गई बावरी। दूर नगरी...

(10)

He lives so far, so far, my friend;
in Gokul I know nothing about.
He lives so far, so far, my friend;
the night brings me fright but
during the day I'm light and bright.
He lives so far, so far, my friend;
with him I feel embarrassed, and
without him I always lose my way.
He lives so far, so far, my friend;
a slow walk with a pitcher sprains my
back but when I rush, I spill and splash.
He lives so far, so far, my friend;
my Lord is Girdhar, says Meera
without him I'm lost, empty, insane.
He lives so far, so far, my friend.

(11)

माई री! मैं तो लियो गोविंदो मोल।
कोई कहै छानै, कोई कहै छुपकै, लियो री बजंता ढोल।
कोई कहै मुहंघो, कोई कहै सुहंगो, लियो री तराजू तोल।
कोई कहै कारो, कोई कहै गोरो, लियो री अमोलिक मोल।
या ही कूं सब जाणत है, लियो री आँखी खोल।
मीरा कूं प्रभु दरसण दीज्यो, पूरब जनम को कोल।

(11)

Mother, I have won Govida in an auction.
Some say I bid openly, the others through
a proxy, and the gossip drums beat and roll.
Some say I bid too high, the others too low
but I know he is worth his weight in gold.
Some say he is too dark, the others too pale
but for me he is my single priceless gem.
They think they know all and everything,
but I ask them to open their eyes and look.
Meera pleads her Lord to show his blessed
face, and keep the promise he last made.

(12)

तुम्हरे कारण सब छोड्या, अब मोहि क्यूं तरसावौ हो।
बिरह-बिथा लागी उर अंतर, सो तुम आय बुझावौ हो॥

अब छोड़त नहिं बड़ै प्रभुजी, हंसकर तुरत बुलावौ हो।
मीरा दासी जनम जनम की, अंग से अंग लगावौ हो॥

(12)

I renounced the world for you,
and you keep me waiting and waiting.
My heart longs to be with you; only you
can douse the fiery flame in me, my love.

Don't desert me now, my Lord,
just smile and call me, and I'll come.
I'm your life-long slave, says Meera
craving to be held close so close, my love.

(13)

मत डारो पिचकारी। मैं सगरी भिजगई सारी॥
जीन डारे सो सनमुख रहायो। नहीं तो मैं देउंगी गारी॥
भर पिचकरी मेरे मुखपर डारी। भीजगई तन सारी॥
लाल गुलाल उडावन लागे। मैं तो मनमें बिचारी॥
मीरा कहे प्रभु गिरिधर नागर। चरनकमल बलहारी॥

(13)

Drop your squirt, and stop
spraying; look, I'm soaking wet.
Squirt if you want but stand face
to face or else I'll shout and swear.
Stop squirting so hard on my face;
don't you see I'm soaking wet?
Spray the red powder as much as you
like: I'm unarmed, weak, and frail.
My Lord is Girdhar, says Meera, I'm ready
to live my life in the shade of his lotus feet.

(14)

पतीया मैं कैशी लीखूं, लीखये न जातरे॥
कलम धरत मेरा कर कांपत। नयनमों रड छायो॥
हमारी बीपत उद्धव देखी जात है। हरीसो कहूं वो जानत है॥
मीरा कहे प्रभु गिरिधर नागर। चरणकमल रहो छाये॥

(14)

I can't write you a letter, my love
because I don't know how to.
As soon as I pick a pen my heart
craves, and my eyes turn blind.
Udhav knows my predicament
he'll tell you about my sorry plight.
Meera says, her Lord is Girdhar, in his
lotus-shadow she is ready to live her life.

(15)

मैं गिरधर के घर जाऊँ।
गिरधर म्हांरो सांचो प्रीतम देखत रूप लुभाऊँ॥
रैण पड़ै तबही उठ जाऊँ भोर भये उठिआऊँ।
रैन दिना वाके संग खेलूं ज्यूं त्यूं ताहि रिझाऊँ॥
जो पहिरावै सोई पहिरूं जो दे सोई खाऊँ।
मेरी उणकी प्रीति पुराणी उण बिन पल न रहाऊँ।
जहाँ बैठावें तितही बैठूं बेचै तो बिक जाऊँ।
मीरा के प्रभु गिरधर नागर बार बार बलि जाऊँ॥

(15)

I have come home to be with Girdhar,
my one true love: to feast on his beauty and charm. I rise
as the night falls, and go to bed when the daybreak dawns;
I flirt with him all night, devising new tricks to excite.
I slip on whatever he offers, and eat whatever he feels right.
Our love is boundless; without him my life has no hope, no light.
He says sit, and I sit; I sell you, he says; I'm sold, I humbly reply.
My Lord is Girdhar, says Meera, for him I am ready to die.

www.ingramcontent.com/pod-product-compliance
Lightning Source LLC
Chambersburg PA
CBHW020331010526
44107CB00054B/2076